The Animal Song

Bullfrog, woodchuck, wolverine, goose,
Whippoorwill, chipmunk, jackal, moose.

Mud turtle, whale, glowworm, bat,
Salamander, snail, Maltese cat.

Black squirrel, coon, opossum, wren,
Red squirrel, loon, South Guinea hen.

Reindeer, blacksnake, crocodile, quail,
Martin, wild drake, nightingale.

House rat, muskrat, brown bear, doe,
Chickadee, peacock, bobolink, crow.

Eagle, kinkajou, mountain goat, widgeon,
Cougar, armadillo, beaver, pigeon.

Little People™ Big Book

About
ANIMALS

TIME LIFE for Children™

Table of Contents

Animals on the Farm

Animals Far Away

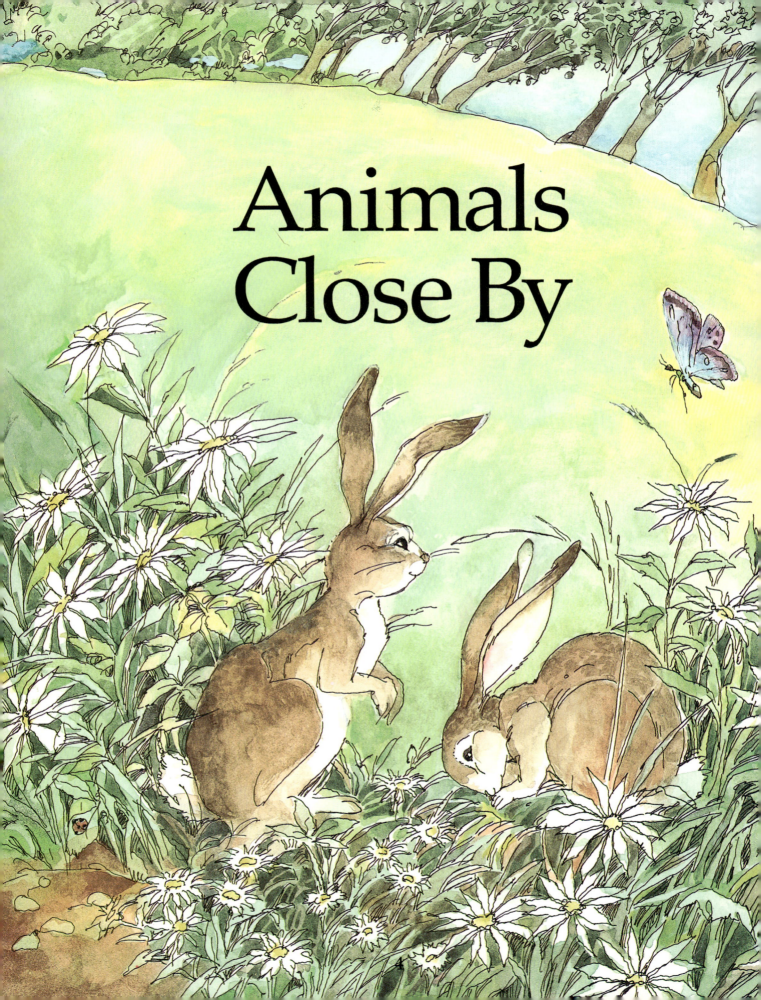

Animals
Close By

Chums

He sits and begs; he gives a paw;
   He is, as you can see,
The finest dog you ever saw,
   And he belongs to me.
He follows everywhere I go
   And even when I swim.
I laugh because he thinks, you know,
   That I belong to him.

Arthur Guiterman

Pete and Bobbit Go Pogo
by Laura Hitchcock

Bobbit was a little white dog. He lived with a small boy named Pete, and they were the best of friends.

Every day, Pete and Bobbit played together, running, jumping, and playing tag. When nighttime came, they curled up on Pete's little bed and snored the night away, still together. They loved each other very much.

None of this was too unusual for a boy and a small dog.

But Bobbit was a *very* unusual dog. That's because he had a very special skill. Pete discovered it one morning when the two went out to play.

"What shall we do first, Bobbit?" asked Pete, yawning. "Run? Jump? Play tag?"

Suddenly, he realized Bobbit was not next to him. He turned around—and there was Bobbit BOINGing and SPROINGing on a pogo stick!

"WowEEE!" cried Pete. He grabbed another pogo stick, and off they went together!

From then on, Bobbit and Pete pogo-ed every day, up and down, down and up, all around the yard. Sometimes their eyes even wiggled for a while after they stopped, because they'd been pogo-ing so long.

Not surprisingly, the neighbors thought this pogo-ing was quite extraordinary. And it made them very happy to watch. "That little dog is so smart!" they would tell each other. "What a pup!"

Pete and Bobbit would smile and wave as they pogo-ed. They loved to see people happy.

Little by little, Bobbit's fame grew. Soon, the neighbors told their friends. The friends told their relatives. The relatives told their pen pals. And when a newspaper reporter interviewed Bobbit, the quote came out on the front page! "'ARF-ARF-*ARF!*' CLAIMS POGO PUP,"
it said.

Soon crowds of people were surrounding Pete's yard to see the famous pup. Letters and postcards began arriving, too—big, gigantic sacks of them. All of them said the same thing! "Please come to our town! We want to see a dog go BOING on a pogo stick!"

But the invitations were for Bobbit only. Pete and Bobbit were sad that they would be apart, but Pete was understanding. After all, lots of little boys know how to pogo. But a *dog* who can pogo is very unusual!

"Bobbit, I'll miss you," said Pete, hugging his friend good-bye. "But just think of all the travel, all the pogo-ing, and all the people you'll make happy."

So, Bobbit traveled all over the country, pogo-ing here and pogo-ing there. He pogo-ed in small towns, big towns, and playgrounds. He pogo-ed in schools, parades, and polka festivals.

Everywhere he went, people laughed and gasped in amazement to see him BOINGing and SPROINGing on a pogo stick. He was the most unusual little dog they had ever seen, and the more he pogo-ed, the happier they got!

There were two, however, who were *not* happy...namely, Bobbit and Pete. There was lots of travel, fame, fun, and pogo-ing for Bobbit, but something was missing. Luckily, Bobbit had a plan.

At the very next show, Bobbit got his usual introduction: "Hurry, hurry! It's the most extraordinary little dog in all the land! The one and only...BOBBIT, THE POGO PUP!"

All eyes turned to Bobbit. But Bobbit just sat there.

One minute passed. Then two. The crowd started whispering.

"What an ordinary little dog! Why are we watching an ordinary dog?"

When people realized Bobbit wouldn't pogo anymore, they sent him home on the bus. Bobbit's plan had worked!

Pete was very happy to see his good friend again. Soon, the two were jumping, running, and playing tag, just like before. At night, they curled up in bed together, just like before.

Finally, they even took out their pogo sticks like before. At first, they pogo-ed cautiously and quietly. Then, a little higher—then higher still. Soon, they were pogo-ing up, down, and all around the yard. BOING! SPROING! Somehow, it was lots more fun now than it had been for either of them for a long, long time.

"Can it be?" cried a neighbor, hurrying out to see. "Bobbit is pogo-ing again?"

Pete looked at Bobbit. Bobbit looked at Pete.

At last, Pete smiled. "Yes, Bobbit is pogo-ing . . . but now we're a team! We only pogo *together!*"

"I see!" said the neighbor, who promptly told his friends. The friends told relatives, and the relatives told their pen pals.

Once again, letters and postcards began to arrive, in gigantic, big sacks. Except now the invitations were for Bobbit *and Pete!*

You see, a dog who can pogo is unusual. But a dog-and-boy pogo team is unusual, too.

And so, Pete and Bobbit BOINGed and SPROINGed all over the world for many years. They traveled, they pogo-ed, and they made lots of people happy.

And neither of them was lonely for a second!

DID YOU EVER WONDER
ABOUT PETS

Why do dogs wag their tails?
Dogs wag their tails from side to side when they are happy. They wag them up and down when they are unhappy. But when a dog is scared, he sticks his tail between his legs.

Do cats have nine lives?
Cats only *seem* to have nine lives. But they're so clever and so nimble that they *are* good at escaping from dangerous situations. Cats run and jump so easily, they can often get away from trouble.

Why do cats have whiskers?
Whiskers that grow on a cat's chin, the sides of its face, and above its eyes help the cat find its way in the dark. They also help to protect its eyes.

Can a turtle leave its shell?

A turtle's shell is part of its body, just as your skin and bones are part of yours. A turtle can't leave its shell, the same way you can't leave your skeleton. Its heavy shell protects the turtle from danger.

Why does a snake always flick its tongue?

A snake's tongue is very sensitive. It can detect noise and movement. Since a snake has no ears, it flicks its tongue to "listen" to its surroundings.

Can a pet fish learn tricks?

You can't teach a pet fish to fetch or to roll over, but you can train it to swim toward you at the side of the tank when you tap on the glass. Gently tap on the glass just before you feed your fish. Soon it will swim toward you *every time* you tap—not just at feeding time.

OH WHERE, OH WHERE HAS MY LITTLE DOG GONE?

Oh where, oh where has my little dog gone?
Oh where, oh where can he be?
With his ears cut short and his tail cut long,
Oh where, oh where can he be?

With so many pooches playing in the park, Marvin can't seem to find his own dog. Maybe you can help him out. Just look for the pup with short ears and a long tail—that's the one!

MY KITTEN GROWS UP

1. One day, about a year ago, my cat Snowball was missing. I thought she was lost! But I found her at last. She was nestled in an old blanket in the closet, surrounded by a litter of just-born kittens! They were all tiny, and they couldn't see or hear. Snowball nursed them, and cleaned them, and kept them warm. They couldn't do anything but mew!

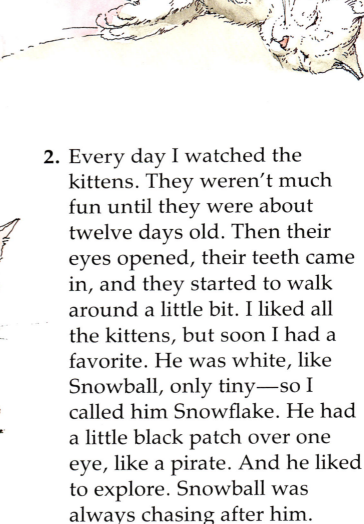

2. Every day I watched the kittens. They weren't much fun until they were about twelve days old. Then their eyes opened, their teeth came in, and they started to walk around a little bit. I liked all the kittens, but soon I had a favorite. He was white, like Snowball, only tiny—so I called him Snowflake. He had a little black patch over one eye, like a pirate. And he liked to explore. Snowball was always chasing after him.

3. Snowflake was my brave little pirate. By the time he was a month old, he had all his kitten teeth. He was the first of the litter to eat real cat food and drink water from a dish. Soon Snowball gave up trying to keep him beside her. Snowflake was just too curious!

4. But Snowflake still had a lot to learn from his mother. She taught him how to wash his face with his paws, how to use the litter box, and how to sharpen his claws on the scratching post. A pirate cat needs sharp claws!

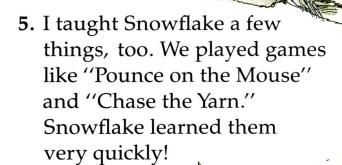

5. I taught Snowflake a few things, too. We played games like "Pounce on the Mouse" and "Chase the Yarn." Snowflake learned them very quickly!

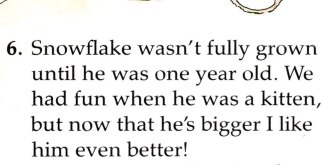

6. Snowflake wasn't fully grown until he was one year old. We had fun when he was a kitten, but now that he's bigger I like him even better!

Joan Israel

15

Missing

Has anybody seen my mouse?
I opened his box for half a minute,
Just to make sure he was really in it,
And while I was looking, he jumped outside!
I tried to catch him, I tried, I tried. . . .
I think he's somewhere about the house.
Has *anyone* seen my mouse?

Uncle John, have you seen my mouse?
Just a small sort of mouse, a dear little brown one,
He came from the country, he wasn't a town one,
So he'll feel all lonely in a London street;
Why, what could he possibly find to eat?

He must be somewhere. I'll ask Aunt Rose:
Have *you* seen a mouse with a woffelly nose?
Oh, somewhere about—
He's just got out. . . .

Hasn't *anybody* seen my mouse?

A.A. Milne

*Do **you** see this poor little boy's lost mouse?*
He's hiding somewhere inside this house.
Where could that little brown country mouse be?
If you look hard enough you will find him—you'll see!

16

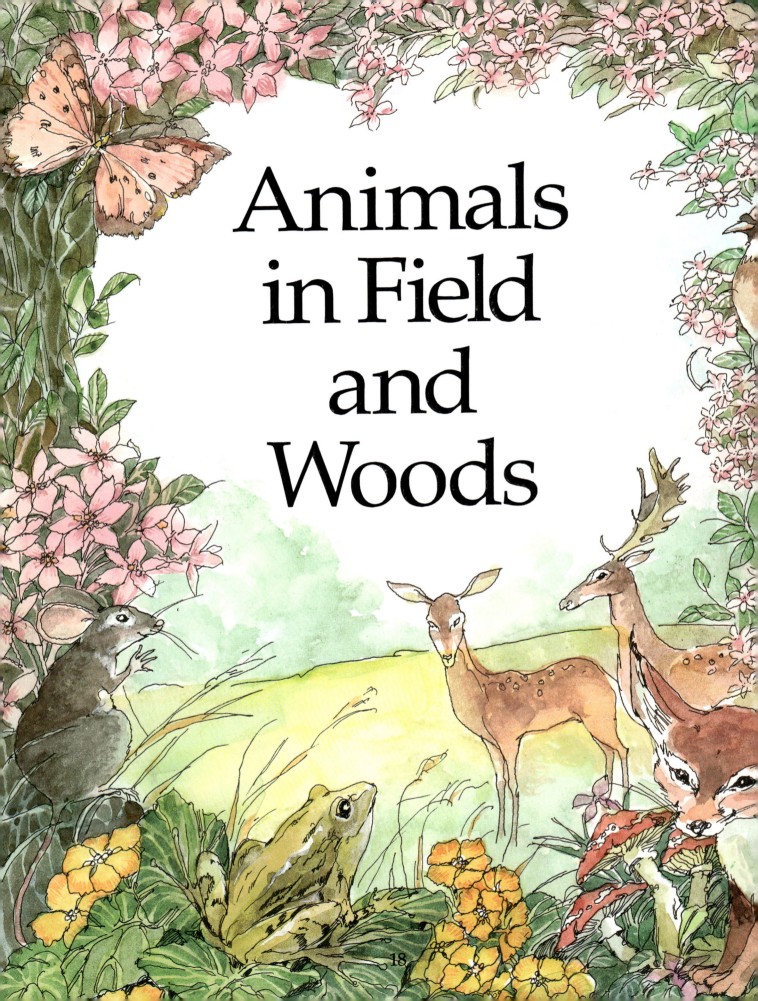

Animals
in Field
and
Woods

Hurt No Living Thing

Hurt no living thing:
Ladybird nor butterfly,
Nor moth with dusty wing,
Nor cricket chirping cheerily,
Nor grasshopper so light of leap,
Nor dancing gnat, nor beetle fat,
Nor harmless worms that creep.

Christina Rossetti

The Tortoise and the Hare

A Retelling of a Famous Fable by Aesop

Tortoise and Hare were friends. They shared a little cottage in the woods, but it wasn't always easy, for they were as different as night and day. Hare was a speedy sort; he liked to do everything fast, but he was careless. Tortoise was just the opposite: he was always careful, but he was slow as molasses. They drove each other crazy.

One morning Tortoise woke up, looked around, and said, "This place is a mess. It's time to do the spring cleaning, Hare."

"I'll do the cleaning," offered Hare, "while you make the soup."

Tortoise slowly got out of bed and began to get dressed. Hare ran around the house picking things up and tossing them into the closet. Tortoise was still brushing his teeth when Hare said, "There. The house is all clean."

Tortoise spit out his toothpaste and sputtered, "You call that clean? All you did was hide everything."

"Don't be so picky, Tortoise," said Hare. "And start the soup, will you? I'm starving."

"You make the soup," Tortoise said. "And I'll *really* clean the house."

While Tortoise scrubbed and swept every inch of the house, Hare dumped some vegetables and water in a pot and turned the heat on high, so the soup would cook faster. Tortoise was just beating the rugs when Hare called, "Soup's on!"

"Doesn't the house look nice now?" asked Tortoise.

"It looks great," said Hare. "How do you do it?"

"You know what I always say," Tortoise answered. "Slow and steady cleans the house."

"Come on, let's eat," said Hare. But when they looked into the pot, all they saw was a bunch of burned vegetables. In his hurry, Hare had turned up the heat too high, and all the water had boiled away. Nothing was left but a sticky, blackened paste.

"You burned the soup, Hare," said Tortoise. "It looks awful!"

"It was an accident," grumbled Hare.

Tortoise started the soup all over again, letting it simmer slowly. Hare was wild with hunger by the time it was done, but he had to admit it was delicious. "What is your recipe, Tortoise?" he asked.

"You know what I always say," said Tortoise. "Slow and steady cooks the soup."

"Well, there's one thing that slow and steady *isn't* any good for," said Hare. "And that's running races."

"Want to bet?" replied Tortoise.

"Okay," said Hare. "I'll bet you another pot of soup I can beat you in a race."

"It's a bet," Tortoise agreed.

Hare and Tortoise decided upon a starting point and a finish line. Their

neighbor Fox agreed to be the judge.

"On your mark, get set, go!" yelled Fox.

Hare raced from the starting line with the speed of lightning. Soon he was over the hill and far away.

Tortoise walked slowly along at his usual pace. He couldn't go much faster than that, anyway.

"Why don't you give up now, Tortoise?" asked Fox. "Hare will win this race easily."

"We'll see," said Tortoise, and he plodded steadily down the road.

Meanwhile, Hare was almost at the finish line. He looked back, but Tortoise was just a tiny dot far behind him. "Poor little guy," said Hare. "It looks as if he'll be making another pot of soup today."

Hare's speedy run had given him an appetite.

"I think I'll go get a carrot burger," he decided. "I'll be back in plenty of time to win the race."

So Hare trotted over to the Badger Diner and sat at the counter.

"What's new, Hare?" asked Badger.

"Listen to this," said Hare. "That stick-in-the-mud Tortoise challenged me to a race today. Isn't that a riot?"

23

Badger laughed, "Yeah, that's a good one."

"He's trudging down the road right now, while I'm sitting here eating carrot burgers! And I'm still going to win! Ha ha ha!"

Hare whiled away the afternoon eating carrot burgers, drinking strawberry shakes, and chatting with Badger. The sun was starting to sink when Badger said, "Hey, Hare, it's getting late. Don't you think you should go finish that race now?"

"Oh my goodness, I lost track of the time!" shouted Hare, as he jumped up to leave. "See you on the victory stand, Badger!"

Hare ran toward the finish line. But when he got closer, he saw that Tortoise was almost there! Hare raced full-speed to catch up—but he was too late. Fox waved the checkered flag. Tortoise had won the race!

"I can't believe it!" cried Hare. He felt a little embarrassed. "How did you do it, Tortoise?"

"Well, you know what I always say . . . ," said Tortoise.

"Don't tell me," mumbled Hare. "'Slow and steady wins the race.'"

"That's right," said Tortoise modestly. "Now, I believe you owe me a pot of soup."

The two friends went home together and Hare cooked Tortoise a pot of soup. But this time he cooked it very, very slowly. And it was the best soup they had ever tasted!

ANIMAL HIDE-AND-SEEK

There are lots of animals hiding in the woods. You can find them all. Point to them as you find them.

- Find four animals that can fly.
- Find seven animals that have fur.
- Which animal has antlers?
- Which is the smallest animal?
- Find four animals in the water.
- Can you find Lucky the dog?

26

Down by the Bay

Down by the bay, where the watermelons grow,
Back to my house I dare not go,
For if I do, my mother will say,
"Did you ever see a moose kissing a goose,
Down by the bay, down by the bay?"

Down by the bay, where the watermelons grow,
Back to my house I dare not go,
For if I do, my mother will say,
"Did you ever see a moose kissing a goose,
Did you ever see a whale with a polka-dot tail,
Down by the bay, down by the bay?"

Down by the bay, where the watermelons grow,
Back to my house I dare not go,
For if I do, my mother will say,
"Did you ever see a moose kissing a goose,
Did you ever see a whale with a polka-dot tail,
Did you ever see a bear combing his hair,
Down by the bay, down by the bay?"

Down by the bay, where the watermelons grow,
Back to my house I dare not go,
For if I do, my mother will say,
"Did you ever see a moose kissing a goose,
Did you ever see a whale with a polka-dot tail,
Did you ever see a bear combing his hair,
Did you ever see llamas eating their pajamas,
Down by the bay, down by the bay?"

Traditional

WINTER SLEEPERS

Each year when winter comes, animals who live outdoors prepare for the cold winter days ahead. Some animals settle down for a few months of rest in their winter quarters. They find hidden, protected places and fall into a sleep so deep it may last all winter. This is called "hibernation."

30

Bats sleep upside down by holding on to something with their hind feet. They sleep through the winter with their wings folded tight to their sides.

Raccoons sleep in cozy tree hollows.

Under the tree, the **woodchuck** or **groundhog** digs a tunnel to his bedroom. Then he seals the door with mud and sleeps away the winter.

The **black bear** sleeps very soundly in his cozy cave. He likes to sleep alone and does not like to be disturbed.

Snakes spend the winter in underground dens. When they sleep, they roll up together in balls to keep warm.

Some **turtles** sleep underground. They sleep in the mud or under tree roots.

The **dormouse** sleeps curled in a ball. She sleeps so soundly she can be rolled across the ground without waking up.

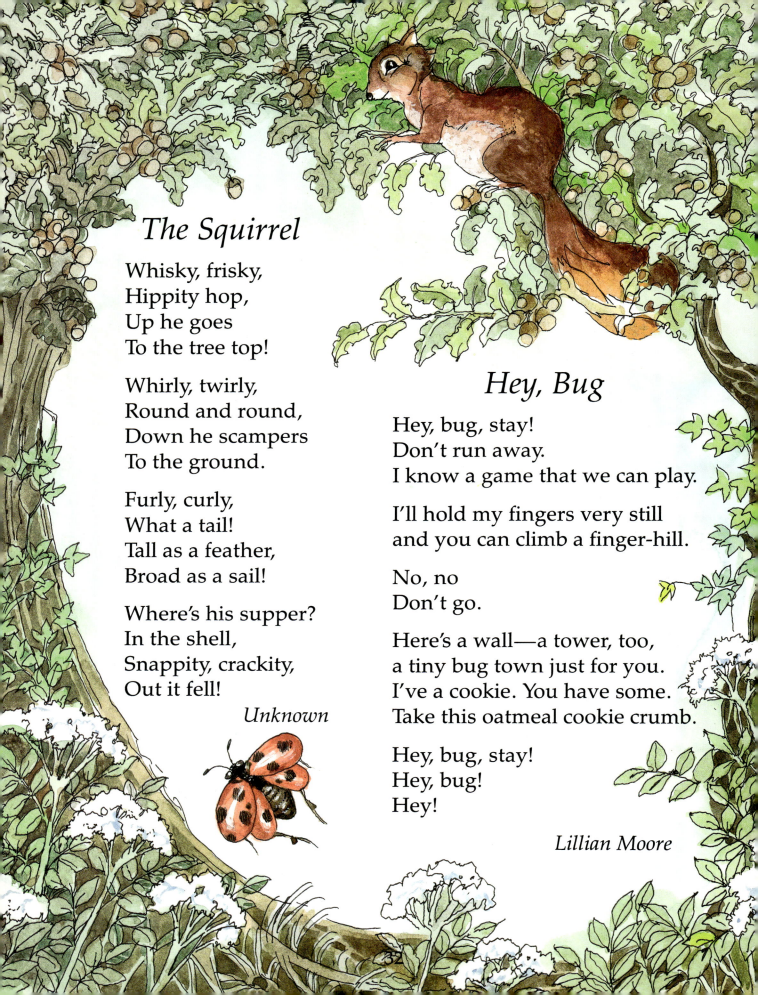

The Squirrel

Whisky, frisky,
Hippity hop,
Up he goes
To the tree top!

Whirly, twirly,
Round and round,
Down he scampers
To the ground.

Furly, curly,
What a tail!
Tall as a feather,
Broad as a sail!

Where's his supper?
In the shell,
Snappity, crackity,
Out it fell!

Unknown

Hey, Bug

Hey, bug, stay!
Don't run away.
I know a game that we can play.

I'll hold my fingers very still
and you can climb a finger-hill.

No, no
Don't go.

Here's a wall—a tower, too,
a tiny bug town just for you.
I've a cookie. You have some.
Take this oatmeal cookie crumb.

Hey, bug, stay!
Hey, bug!
Hey!

Lillian Moore

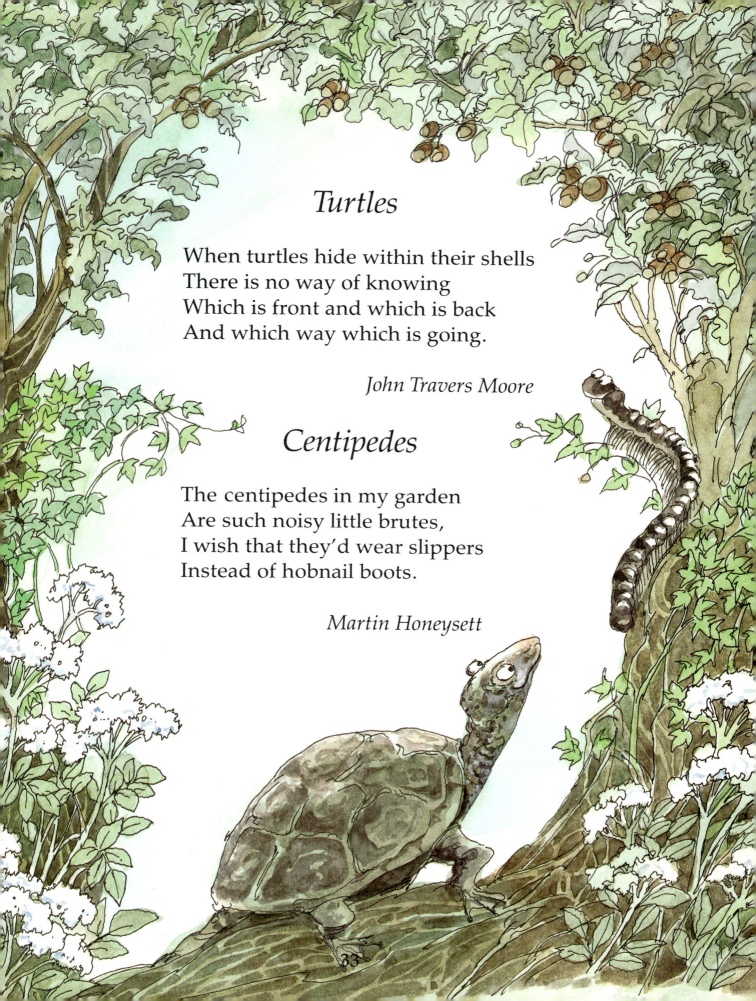

Turtles

When turtles hide within their shells
There is no way of knowing
Which is front and which is back
And which way which is going.

John Travers Moore

Centipedes

The centipedes in my garden
Are such noisy little brutes,
I wish that they'd wear slippers
Instead of hobnail boots.

Martin Honeysett

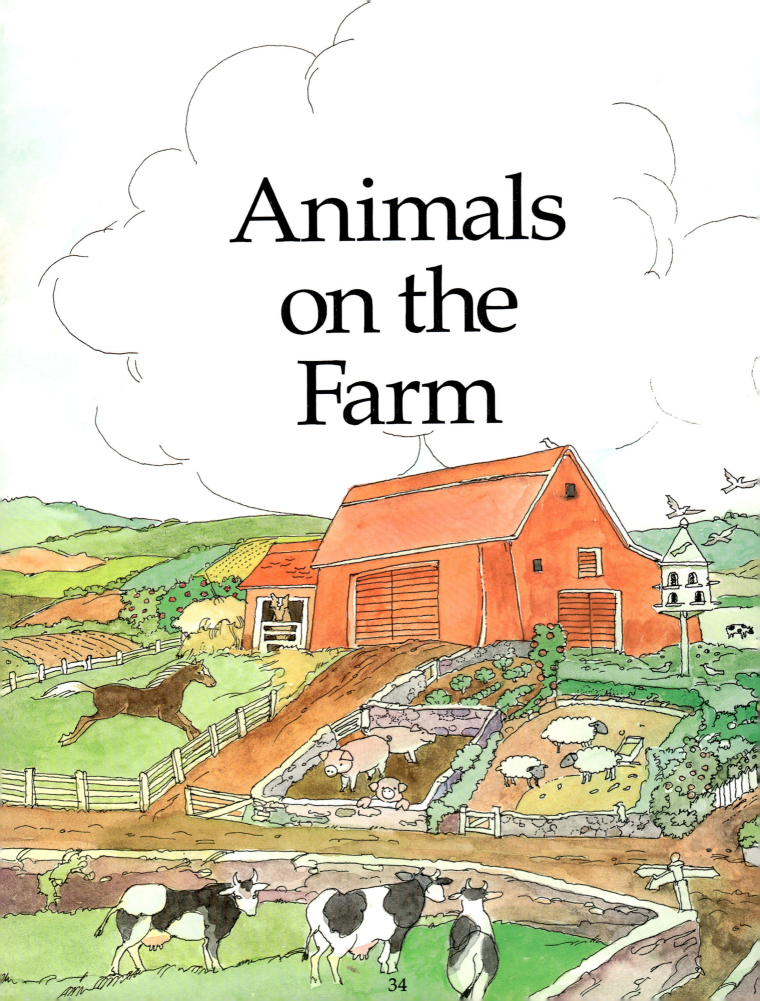

Animals on the Farm

Farm Life

I love to go to see Aunt Flo
And chase her old fat hen
That wobbles all around the yard
Again and then again!

I love to watch the piggies eat
And hear the horses neigh,
And run the little calves a race
And slide down stacks of hay.

And when I'm dusted up a lot
And sort of skinned my knees,
I like to go inside and rest,
And have some milk and cheese.

Ruth Edna Stanton

OLD MACDONALD HAD A FARM

Here's a fun new way to sing an old song. When you see a picture of an animal, sing out the animal's name. Then, when the time comes, sing the sound the animal makes.

Old MacDonald had a farm,
Ee-yi-ee-yi-oh!
And on that farm he had a 🐷,

Ee-yi-ee-yi-oh!

With an *oink* *oink* here,

And an *oink* *oink* there,

Here an *oink*, there an *oink*,

Everywhere an *oink* *oink*.

Old MacDonald had a farm,
Ee-yi-ee-yi-oh!

Old MacDonald had a farm,
Ee-yi-ee-yi-oh!
And on that farm he had a ,

Ee-yi-ee-yi-oh!

With a moo moo here,
And a moo moo there,
Here a moo, there a moo,
Everywhere a moo moo.

Old MacDonald had a farm,
Ee-yi-ee-yi-oh!

Old MacDonald had a farm,
Ee-yi-ee-yi-oh!
And on that farm he had a ,

Ee-yi-ee-yi-oh!

With a baa baa here,
And a baa baa there,
Here a baa, there a baa,
Everywhere a baa baa.

Old MacDonald had a farm,
Ee-yi-ee-yi-oh!

Old MacDonald had a farm,
Ee-yi-ee-yi-oh!
And on that farm he had a ,

Ee-yi-ee-yi-oh!

With a neigh neigh here,
And a neigh neigh there,
Here a neigh, there a neigh,
Everywhere a neigh neigh.

Old MacDonald had a farm,
Ee-yi-ee-yi-oh!

37

The Little Red Hen
A Retelling of a Traditional Tale

One morning, as the Little Red Hen was walking through the barnyard with her three little chicks and her friends—the dog, the duck, and the pig—she saw some grains of wheat on the ground.

"Who will help me plant this wheat?" she asked.

"Not I," said the dog. "I'm too tired."
"Not I," said the duck. "I'm too important."
"Not I," said the pig. "I'm too hungry."

"Then I will plant it myself," said the Little Red Hen. All summer long she cared for the wheat. She watered and weeded and watched it grow tall.

When the wheat was ready to be cut, the Little Red Hen asked her friends,

"Who will help me cut this wheat?"

"Not I," said the dog, as he lounged lazily on the ground.
"Not I," said the duck, as he puffed up his chest feathers.
"Not I," said the pig, as he munched on a corn cob.

"Then I will cut the wheat myself," said the Little Red Hen. And she cut the wheat and put it in a wheelbarrow.

When all the wheat was cut and ready to be threshed, the Little Red Hen asked,
"Who will help me thresh the wheat?"

"Not I," said the dog, yawning and stretching.
"Not I," said the duck, as he straightened his posture.
"Not I," said the pig, as he swallowed an apple.

"Then I will thresh the wheat myself," said the Little Red Hen.

Soon the wheat was cut and threshed. The Little Red Hen put all the wheat into a sack to take to the mill.

"Who will help me take the wheat to the mill?" asked the Little Red Hen.

"Not I," said the dog, as he sleepily rubbed his eyes.
"Not I," said the duck, as he held his head high.
"Not I," said the pig, as he slurped up some ice cream.

"Then I will take it myself," said the Little Red Hen. So off she went to the mill.

When she came back with the flour, the Little Red Hen asked, "Who will help me bake bread with the flour?"

"Not I," said the dog, laying down for a nap.
"Not I," said the duck, as he brushed off his tail.
"Not I," said the pig, as he polished off some scraps.

"Then I will bake the bread myself," she said.

So the Little Red Hen baked the bread all by herself. She mixed and kneaded the dough. Then she shaped it into two big loaves of bread and set them on the window sill to rise. When the loaves had risen, she baked them in the oven. Soon the bread was done, and the Little Red Hen asked,

"Who will help me eat this bread?"

"I will," said the dog, forgetting how tired he was.
"I will," said the duck, forgetting how important he was.
"I will," said the pig, remembering how hungry he was.

But the Little Red Hen shook her head.

"No, you won't," said the Little Red Hen.
I planted the wheat all by myself.
I cut the wheat all by myself.
I threshed the wheat all by myself.
I took the wheat to the mill all by myself.
I baked the bread all by myself.
"And now, I'm going to eat the bread. . .with my own little chicks."

And the Little Red Hen and her chicks did just that!

HAPPY BIRTHDAY!

These farm babies have just been born.
Hello, babies!

A new baby calf
needs a bath.
Mother cow cleans him
with her tongue.
Cows have one baby
at a time.

This little foal
tries to stand up
on her wobbly legs.
When she is big
she will run like lightning!
But first she has to get used
to her long, long legs.

Baby lamb stands up right away
to find his mother's udder.
His little tail wiggles
when he drinks.
Soon he'll be full.

Mother hen must sit on her eggs
to keep them warm.
Then each baby chick will
peck, peck, peck—
until he is out of his shell.
On the first day,
the chick learns who his mother is.
He follows her everywhere!

Pigs have big families. During the first few days, piglets
fight for the best nipple. Then they always go to the same
one. But when they are full, they all fall asleep.
Good night, babies!

FAVORITE MOTHER GOOSE RHYMES

Higgledy Piggledy

Higgledy piggledy,
My black hen,
She lays eggs for gentlemen:
Sometimes nine and sometimes ten.
Higgledy Piggledy,
My black hen!

To Market, To Market

To market, to market, to buy a fat pig.
Home again, home again, jiggety jig.
To market, to market, to buy a fat hog.
Home again, home again, jiggety jog.
To market, to market, to buy a plum bun.
Home again, home again, market is done.

Little Bo-Peep

Little Bo-Peep has lost her sheep,
And can't tell where to find them.
Leave them alone and they'll come home,
Wagging their tails behind them.

Animals Far Away

Donkey Riding

Were you ever in Quebec,
Stowing timbers on a deck,
Where there's a king in his golden crown,
Riding on a donkey?

Hey ho, and away we go,
Donkey riding, donkey riding.
Hey ho, and away we go,
Riding on a donkey.

Were you ever in Cardiff Bay,
Where the folks all shout "Hooray"?
Here comes John with his three months' pay,
Riding on a donkey.

Hey ho, and away we go,
Donkey riding, donkey riding.
Hey ho, and away we go,
Riding on a donkey.

Were you ever off Cape Horn,
Where it's always fine and warm?
See the lion and the unicorn,
Riding on a donkey.

Hey ho, and away we go,
Donkey riding, donkey riding.
Hey ho, and away we go,
Riding on a donkey.

Traditional

DID YOU EVER WONDER
ABOUT WILD ANIMALS

Why do elephants have trunks?
An elephant's trunk is very useful. The elephant uses it to gather leaves to eat and to spray water on its back like a shower.

Why do ostriches bury their heads in the sand?
The ostrich does not really bury its head in the sand. What it is really doing is digging a hole in the sand with its beak. The hole will become a nest for its eggs.

48

Why do monkeys have long tails?
Monkeys use their tails for balance when they jump or swing from tree to tree. Sometimes they can grasp branches with their tails.

Why do giraffes have long necks?
The giraffe likes to eat leaves from the tops of trees.
It needs a long neck to help it reach the leaves.

Why do leopards have spots?
The leopard's spots help it to hide from danger. They make the leopard very hard to see in a leafy forest.

How the Elephant Got Its Trunk

A Retelling of the Story
by Rudyard Kipling

Did you know that a long, long time ago, elephants had no trunks, just bumps where their trunks should have been? This is a story about how elephants finally got their trunks.

Once there was a Baby Elephant who sometimes asked too many questions. He asked questions about what he saw, or heard, or smelled, or felt, or touched. But the question he most frequently asked, which, by the way, got him into the most trouble, was, "What does the crocodile eat for breakfast?"

First, Baby Elephant went to see his Uncle Giraffe, who had his head high in the trees as he ate green leaves.

"Oh, excuse me, Uncle Giraffe, sir," called the Baby Elephant politely. "Could you please tell me what the crocodile eats for breakfast?"

"Don't *ever* ask me that question!" shouted Uncle Giraffe. Then he spanked the Baby Elephant!

So the Baby Elephant went to see his Aunt Hippopotamus, who was taking a bath in a big, warm lake.

"Excuse me, Auntie," called the Baby Elephant.

"Yes, sweetheart?" replied Aunt Hippopotamus. "What can I do for you?"

"What does the crocodile eat for breakfast?" asked Baby Elephant, ever so sweetly.

Aunt Hippopotamus slowly rose out of the water, causing a small tidal wave.

"Don't *ever* ask me that question!" she shouted. Then she gave him a good, wet spanking for asking such nonsensical questions.

So Baby Elephant went to see his best friend, the Kolokolo Bird.
"Could you *please* tell me what the crocodile eats for breakfast?" he asked.

The Kolokolo Bird told him, "Go to the banks of the great, gray-green, greasy Limpopo River, where the crocodile lives, and ask him for yourself."

What a good idea, thought Baby Elephant. The very next morning, he took a lunch of one hundred pounds of short, red bananas, one hundred pounds of long, purple sugarcane, and seventeen green, crackly melons, and set off for the great, gray-green, greasy Limpopo River.

Eventually, Baby Elephant came to the banks of the Limpopo River and sat down to eat his lunch. He had eaten all of the bananas and half of the sugarcane, when suddenly a huge crocodile with a long snout came out of the water.

"Are you a crocodile?" asked Baby Elephant, who had never seen a crocodile before.

"Yes," replied the crocodile, and he wept a few crocodile tears to show it was quite true. "What can I do for you?"

The Baby Elephant grew all breathless and panted with excitement. He kneeled down close to the crocodile and asked, "What do you eat for breakfast?"

"Come closer and I'll whisper in your ear," replied the crocodile, winking one eye.

Baby Elephant put his nose really close to the crocodile's musky, tusky mouth. SNAP! The crocodile caught Baby Elephant by his little nose and held tight. Through his teeth, he said, "I think today I'll eat *Baby Elephant* for breakfast!"

Baby Elephant was very much surprised, and really annoyed. "Let go!" he yelled. Then he set his legs and pulled and pulled as hard as he could.

Well, soon the strangest thing happened. Baby Elephant's nose began to stretch just like bubble gum. In fact, it grew quite long. Finally the crocodile had to let go and fell back into the Limpopo River with a loud PLOP!

"That was close," said Baby Elephant aloud. Then he saw his nose. "Oh, *my*," he said, "what an awful, ugly, useless nose!" And he sat down to wait for his nose to shrink.

While he waited, a fly came up and stung him. Without thinking twice, Baby Elephant swatted that fly dead with his new long nose. "Hmmm," said Baby Elephant. "I could never do that with a mere-smear nose!"

Baby Elephant then picked a lovely bunch of ripe bananas off a tall tree. Then, just for fun, he schlooped up a schloop of mud and slapped it on his head. This new nose was terrific!

"This is fun!" shouted Baby Elephant, and he lifted his new nose and let out a wondrous noise. It was as loud as a trumpet! Then he marched home with his new nose proudly held high. He would show his relatives all the new things he could do.

When the Baby Elephant's family saw his new nose, they fell silent and circled around him, amazed.

"Where did you get such a beautiful nose?" they finally asked.

Baby Elephant told everyone about the crocodile. So all the other elephants romped and stomped over to the wide, muddy banks of the great, gray-green, greasy Limpopo River to get their noses stretched, too.

Well, now you know why elephants have trunks today. At least, that's the story, if you believe it.

BIG AND SMALL ANIMALS

There are great big animals and there are small animals. How big is big?
How small is small? Take a look and see...

Elephants are bigger than people.

An elephant weighs more than a whole classroom of children.

But a blue whale is bigger than an elephant. The blue whale is the biggest animal of all.

Some dogs are bigger than people.

Some dogs are smaller than a baby.

A mouse is smaller than the smallest dog.
What's smaller than a mouse? All insects are smaller than
mice. A bug is smaller than a mouse.

WILD, WILD ANIMAL RIDDLES!

What animal is always laughing? The happy-potamus! *And you'll laugh, too, when you read these wild, wild animal riddles!*

Where do wild animals like to play?
On the jungle gym!

With what big cat should you never play cards?
The cheetah!

Where do little bears sit on the train?
In the cub-oose!

What is the largest mouse in the world?
A hippopota-mouse!

Why do lions roar?
They would feel silly saying "Oink!"

What business did the father ape want his son to go into?
The monkey business!

What happened when the tiger ate a lemon?
He became a sour puss!

When do giraffes have eight legs?
When there are two of them!

What is bigger than an elephant but lighter than a feather?
An elephant's shadow!

What's the best year for a kangaroo?
Leap year!

Why do lions eat raw meat?
Because they don't know how to cook!

Ping Ping Finds a Friend

by Shirley Albert

Ping Ping was a happy little panda. He loved to climb trees and tumble head over heels through the bamboo forest where he lived, high up in the mountains of China. Ping Ping loved the cool winds there and the moist mountain air, too. But most of all, he loved to play with his mother.

"There you are, Ping Ping!" Mama Panda always said when the two played hide-and-seek, and together they would scramble through the forest, laughing and having fun. Ping Ping thought he could never be happier.

But then one morning Mama Panda said, "I am much too tired to play today, Ping Ping. Maybe we'll play tomorrow." And she curled up under a tall pine tree and fell asleep.

Ping Ping got up bright and early the next morning, ready to play. But once again, all his mother wanted to do was rest.

Day by day, Mama Panda seemed to need more and more sleep. And day by day, Ping Ping grew sadder and lonelier. Even when his mother wasn't too tired to play, she was suddenly much too busy, gathering bamboo and singing to herself.

Ping Ping decided he needed a friend. So one fine day he set out on a little walk. He soon came to a small clearing.

There, munching on some grass, was a family of yaks.

"Maybe these yaks will be my friends," thought Ping Ping. He

60

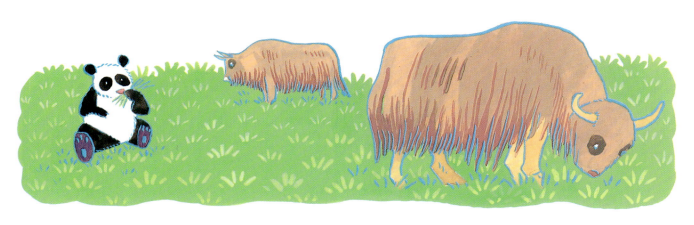

took a deep breath and said, ''Hello there, yaks! May I play with you?''

''Sure!'' said the yaks. ''Won't you join us for lunch? There's nothing we love better than fresh grass.''

''Well, I usually eat bamboo,'' said Ping Ping. ''But I'd like to try your food, too.''

Ping Ping bent down and took a big bite of grass. He munched, and he munched, and he munched. The yaks were watching him closely to see how he liked their food. Ping Ping didn't think the grass was tasty at all, but he bravely swallowed the mouthful he had taken and smiled at the yaks.

''Delicious!'' said Ping Ping, trying to be polite. But then: ''Achoo!'' Ping Ping sneezed and tumbled onto the grass. ''Achoo!'' He sneezed and coughed, tumbling right into a yak's leg. Ouch! Grass definitely did not agree with Ping Ping.

''Are you okay?'' asked the yaks. ''You'd better go home and take care of yourself.''

And so, scratching and sneezing and coughing up a storm, Ping Ping slowly went home.

By the next day, Ping Ping had stopped sneezing, but he still felt lonely. His mother went to sleep right after breakfast, so Ping Ping set off again in search of a friend.

Ping Ping walked and walked until he came to a rushing waterfall. Four leopard cubs were playing nearby. They were rolling around and around, and chasing each other's tails.

''Maybe these leopards will be my friends,'' thought Ping Ping. He took a deep breath and said, ''Hello, leopards! May I play with you?''

''Sure!'' said the leopards. ''Let's play tag! *You're it!*''

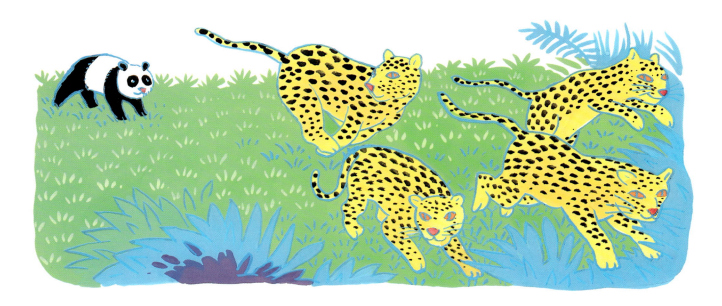

All the leopards quickly darted away from Ping Ping. He lumbered after them, trying to tag them, but they were too quick for a roly-poly panda like Ping Ping. Soon, they were out of sight. From far away, Ping Ping heard one leopard call to another, "Where is that panda? Why isn't he tagging us?"

Ping Ping sighed and started for home. "With no friends to tag, I'll be *it* forever!" he thought.

On his way home, Ping Ping came upon a flock of birds. "Maybe these birds will be my friends," he thought. He took a deep breath, ran up to a bird, touched its wing, and cried, "You're it!"

"What a strange panda!" exclaimed the bird. The whole flock was so startled, they flapped their wings and flew away.

As he watched them go, Ping Ping felt sadder and lonelier than ever. "I guess I'm just no good at making friends," he thought as he trudged home.

Ping Ping decided not to try making any more friends. He passed the time nibbling on bamboo and playing games by himself.

But he was still sad and lonely.

Then one morning Ping Ping was awakened by the sound of his mother's voice. "I have a surprise for you," she whispered.

Ping Ping opened his eyes and saw his mother holding a baby panda. "Come meet your new sister," she said. "Her name is Yu Yu."

Ping Ping softly patted Yu Yu's tiny head. Yu Yu smiled at him. Now he understood why his mother had been too tired and busy to play. She had been getting ready to have a baby, a new friend for Ping Ping!

"*Hooray!*" Ping Ping shouted.

The news of Yu Yu's birth spread quickly throughout the bamboo forest. Soon the yaks, the leopards, and the birds came around to meet Ping Ping's new little sister.

Ping Ping introduced her to them all. "When you are bigger, we will all play together," Ping Ping told Yu Yu.

And they did.

Little People™ Big Book About ANIMALS

TIME-LIFE for CHILDREN™

Publisher: Robert H. Smith
Editorial Director: Neil Kagan
Associate Editor: Jean Burke Crawford
Marketing Director: Ruth P. Stevens
Promotion Director: Kathleen B. Tresnak
Associate Promotion Director: Jane B. Welihozkiy
Production Manager: Prudence G. Harris
Editorial Consultants: Jacqueline A. Ball
Sara Mark

FISHER-PRICE™

Director of Licensed Products: Edward P. Powderly
Marketing Manager, Licensed Products: Ronni Pollack
Product Approval Manager: Mary Ann Bittner
Licensing Administrator: Irwin Katzmann II

PRODUCED BY PARACHUTE PRESS, INC.

Editorial Director: Joan Waricha
Editors: Christopher Medina, Jane Stine
Writers: Noelle Anderson, Shirley Albert,
Laura Hitchcock, Joan Israel,
Grace Maccarone, Natalie Standiford,
Jean Waricha
Designer: Deborah Michel
Illustrators: Yvette Banek, Paul Richer, John Speirs

Time-Life Books Inc. is a wholly owned subsidary
of Time Incorporated.

TIME-LIFE is a trademark of Time Incorporated
U.S.A.

FISHER-PRICE, LITTLE PEOPLE and AWNING
DESIGN are trademarks of Fisher-Price, division of
Quaker Oats Company and are used under license.

Time-Life Books Inc. offers a wide range of fine
publications, including home video products. For
subscription information, call 1-800-621-7026, or
write TIME-LIFE BOOKS, P.O.Box C-32068, Rich-
mond, Virginia 23261-2068.

ACKNOWLEDGMENTS

Every effort has been made to trace the ownership of all copyrighted material and to secure the necessary
permissions to reprint these selections. If any question arises as to the use of any material, the editor and the
publisher, while expressing regret for any inadvertent error, will make the necessary correction in future
printings.

Grateful acknowledgment is made to the following for permission to reprint copyrighted material: Atheneum
Publishers (an imprint of Macmillan Publishing Co.) for ''Hey Bug'' from I FEEL THE SAME WAY by Lilian
Moore, copyright © 1967 by Lilian Moore. EP Dutton, a division of Penguin Books USA, Inc. for ''Missing''
from WHEN WE WERE VERY YOUNG by A.A. Milne, copyright © 1924 by EP Dutton, renewed 1952 by
A.A. Milne. McClelland & Stewart Ltd. for Canadian rights to ''Missing'' by A.A. Milne, copyright © 1952 by
A.A. Milne. Methuen Children's Books for ''Centipedes'' from ANIMAL NONSENSE RHYMES by Martin
Honeysett, copyright © 1984 by Martin Honeysett; and United Kingdom rights to ''Missing'' from WHEN WE
WERE VERY YOUNG by A.A. Milne, copyright © 1952 by A.A. Milne. John Travers Moore for ''Turtles''
from TOWN AND COUNTRYSIDE POEMS, published by Albert Whitman & Co., copyright © 1968 by John
Travers Moore. Louise H. Sclove for ''Chums'' from THE LAUGHING MUSIC by Arthur Guiterman.

Library of Congress Cataloging-in-Publication Data

Little people big book about animals.
    p. cm.
    Summary: A collection of traditional, original, and non-fiction stories, questions and answers, poems, songs,
games, and activities associated with animals.
    ISBN 0-8094-7450-6.—ISBN 0-8094-7451-4 (lib. bdg.)
    1. Animals—Literary collections. [1. Animals—Literary collections.] I. Time-Life Books.
PZ10.3.L7236 1989   89-5078
808.8'99282—dc20   CIP
                                                                                                        AC

TIME-LIFE BOOKS
ALEXANDRIA, VIRGINIA

The Animal Song

Bullfrog, woodchuck, wolverine, goose,
Whippoorwill, chipmunk, jackal, moose.

Mud turtle, whale, glowworm, bat,
Salamander, snail, Maltese cat.

Black squirrel, coon, opossum, wren,
Red squirrel, loon, South Guinea hen.

Reindeer, blacksnake, crocodile, quail,
Martin, wild drake, nightingale.

House rat, muskrat, brown bear, doe,
Chickadee, peacock, bobolink, crow.

Eagle, kinkajou, mountain goat, widgeon,
Cougar, armadillo, beaver, pigeon.